People and places

Bobbie Kalman

The In My World Series

Crabtree Publishing Company

The In My World Series:
Created by Bobbie Kalman

Editor-in-Chief:
Bobbie Kalman

Writing team:
Bobbie Kalman
Janine Schaub
Liz Hart

Researchers:
Colin Ellis
Brian Dore
Bruce Parkinson
Stephanie Gould
Rodney Palmer

Design and mechanicals:
Halina Below-Spada

Illustrations:
Title page and page 31 by Karen Harrison
Pages 2-27 and cover © Mitchell Beazley Publishers 1982
Pages 28 and 29 by Halina Below-Spada © Crabtree
Publishing 1987

Typesetting:
Jay Tee Graphics Ltd.

Cataloguing in Publication Data

Kalman, Bobbie
  People and places

(The In my world series)
ISBN 0-86505-079-1 (hardcover)
ISBN 0-86505-101-1 (softcover)

1. Human settlements - Juvenile literature.
2. Community life - Juvenile literature.
I. Title. II. Series

IIT65.K34 1987   j307

**For Suhartini,
our foster daughter in Indonesia**

350 Fifth Avenue
Suite 3308
New York, N.Y. 10118

120 Carlton Street
Suite 309
Toronto, Ontario
Canada M5A 4K2

Contents

People

There are millions of people all over the world. You can find them in deserts, on islands and mountains, beside oceans, and in villages, towns, and cities. All these people are the same in many ways. Even though they live in different places, they have many of the same needs. They need to eat, drink, and sleep. They need to have shelter, and they need to feel safe and loved. The people in this picture are enjoying many of the same things. They are all outside in the fresh air, exercising and having fun.

Although people have many similarities, they are also very different. No two people on earth look, act, or think in exactly the same way. Each person is unique. The people in this park have their own hopes and dreams for the future.

All over the world, people speak different languages, have different customs, and enjoy different foods and music. All these things are important in shaping the way people act and live.

This book has stories about people who live in interesting places all over the world. Some of the people in these stories may have many things in common with you, while others have a very different way of life. These similarities and differences make our world an exciting place!

City living

The Jacksons moved to this city a week ago. Before they moved here, they lived on a farm. Now Mr. and Mrs. Jackson and their children, Jackie, James, and little Steven, have an apartment on the third floor of this building.

It's a busy Saturday in the Jacksons' new neighborhood. A washing machine is being delivered, and Mrs. Jackson is showing the delivery person where it should go. Mrs. Capella, one of the neighbors, is watching the activities from her window. Some children have come across the street to look at the delivery truck. Maybe James and Jackie will meet them and make new friends!

The Jacksons are sad about leaving their farm, but they are excited about living in the city. They are looking forward to exploring their new neighborhood and visiting the science center, theaters, and shopping centers. Jackie can't wait to start gymnastics lessons, and James wants to visit the museum and see the dinosaurs. Life in the city will be different from life on the farm, but the Jacksons hope it will be just as much fun!

Picture talk

What changes will the Jacksons have in their lives now that they live in the city? What is special about living in the city? Why might the Jacksons miss living in the country?

6

Village living

It's Saturday afternoon and the village is full of activity! Mrs. Gunther and her son Otto have just bought some vegetables from Mrs. Wagner, the grocer. They exchanged the latest village news with Mrs. Wagner as they shopped. On the way home, the Gunthers say hello to several neighbors.

If you lived in this village, you would never be a stranger — everyone would know you! Many of the people who live here were born here and have lived here all their lives. Their parents and grandparents were born here, too. The villagers are proud of their village because their families are part of its history.

The church is the most important building in this community. There are religious services on Sundays and, on the other nights of the week, the church is used for events such as meetings, rehearsals, dances, and bazaars. Otto has just joined a model-making club that meets at the church. He is looking forward to going to his first meeting next week.

Picture talk

Name some of the occupations the village people might have.
What are some of the interesting things you could do if you lived in this village?
What might a child's chores be?

It's sheep-shearing time!

The Kelman family owns and operates a sheep *station*, in Australia. They raise sheep that produce fine wool. This wool is used to make sweaters and blankets.

It is shearing time on the station. Two shearers and some other helpers have been hired to lend a hand. Eve Kelman is helping to bring the sheep, one by one, into the shearing shed. The shearers use electric scissors called *clippers* to cut off the wooly coat in one piece. James is *picker-up*. He sweeps up the wool that has fallen onto the floor. His sister Jane sends the freshly shorn sheep back to the fields. The sheep are happy to be rid of their heavy coats now that summer has come!

Bob and Bill are busy sorting the wool, and Hilary is bundling it into bags. The red truck is leaving with a load of wool. This wool will soon be shipped to countries all over the world.

Sheep farming is hard work, but the Kelmans like animals and enjoy working outdoors. When the shearing is finished, the Kelmans will have a party to celebrate a job well done!

Picture talk
Shearing doesn't hurt the sheep. How do you think it feels?
Why do the shearers need strong arms?
What job do you think this dog has?

A maritime community

Look at all the boats! This seaside town is a popular place in the summer. Some of these sailboats belong to the people who live in town. Others belong to people who have sailed here to visit. When a boat sails into port, the crew members often buy groceries and souvenirs and eat in the restaurants. The money spent by these visitors helps the people of this small community make a living.

The people who live in this port town have several different occupations. Some are store owners, some work with tourists, and some are part of the fishing industry. The men and women who fish leave the harbor early in the morning while it is still dark. They travel out to sea and set their nets and lobster traps. After several hours, they haul in their catch and head back to port. They sometimes sell their fish on the dock, but most of it goes to a nearby factory where it is frozen or packed in cans.

The children in this town love to watch the boats come and go in the harbor. Sometimes they help the sailors by tying the line from a boat to its *mooring ring*.

Picture talk

Some boats have tires or white plastic objects hanging overboard. What are they for?
How is this harbor protected from the ocean?

Roula's island

There is a girl named Roula who lives on this island. Her parents own a boat that takes tourists on sightseeing tours. Roula likes to meet the tourists who come to visit. She talks to them when they ride on her parents' boat.

Roula's uncle is a fisherman. After school, Roula and her brother Ari often help their uncle repair his fishing nets. Sometimes they all go on fishing trips together. Roula is learning how to steer the boat and how to clean squid. She likes to take fresh squid home for her family's dinner.

Sometimes Roula's family visits the mainland to shop for food that can't be bought on the island. Roula enjoys visiting the mainland, but she is always happy to return to her island home. Roula and her family hope their island will always stay as beautiful as it is now. Although they like to show their island to tourists, they do not want big hotels or apartments built on it. All the people who live here love this island just the way it is!

Picture talk

Why do the *residents* of this island like to live here?
Why might the people who live on a small island feel closer to their neighbors than the people who live in a big city?
Why does this island attract visitors?

14

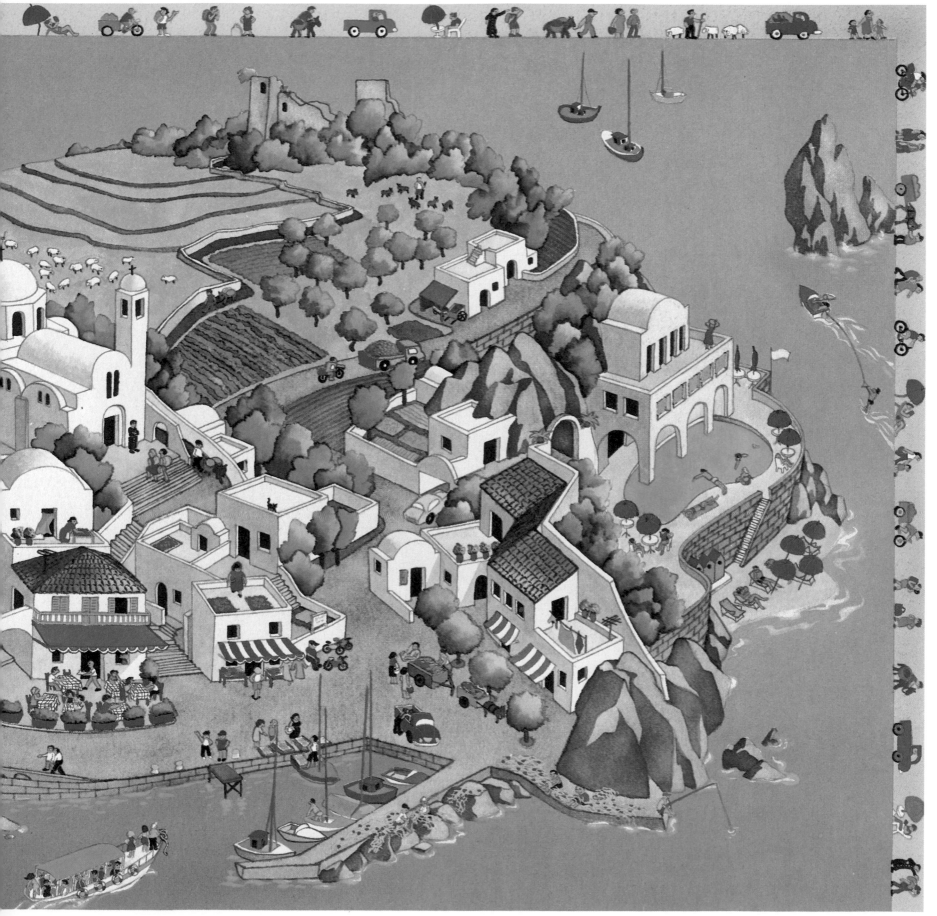

15

Living in the mountains

It's market day! The people walking down this steep path have come from a village high in the mountains of Peru. These villagers are taking their bundles of wool, cotton, and cheese to the marketplace in the village below. There they will trade their goods for items such as rice, sugar, and potatoes.

Some of the mountain villagers use llamas to carry their bundles along the steep and rocky paths. The sure-footed llamas know where to walk so they won't stumble and fall.

Alpacas are animals that look similar to llamas. Both alpacas and llamas provide the mountain villagers with wool to make warm clothes. Alpaca and llama wool is dyed bright colors and woven into cozy sweaters and *ponchos*.

High up in the mountains, it is hard to breathe because there is less *oxygen* in the air. Mountain people have *adapted* to this mountain air. With each breath, a mountain person can absorb more oxygen than a person who lives in the lowland.

Picture talk

What are some differences between the clothes you wear and the clothes the Peruvians are wearing?
There are some fields on the mountainside. Why would farmers plant vegetables there?

17

The dry season is here!

The dry season has come to this tropical village. Not long ago, it was raining all day long, and the river was full. Now it hasn't rained in weeks. It may not rain again for six months! In the distance, the hills have all turned yellow and brown.

People who live in the tropics must prepare themselves for the dry season. During the wet season when there is heavy rain, they collect rainwater in tanks. This water can then be used during the dry season when there is no rain. Sometimes during the dry season, there are so few green plants growing on the ground that the farmers must chop down tree branches so the cows and goats can eat the leaves.

These farmers are harvesting corn that was grown during the wet season. Some fields in this picture have been left *fallow*. A fallow field has no crops planted in it. The soil must rest so it can regain the nutrients that the crops need in order to grow.

During this season, fire is a great threat. A fire that starts can spread quickly through the dry grasses and crops, and with little water, it is very difficult to put it out!

Picture talk

What are some of the ways people are using water?

Look at the river and the bridge. What clues tell you that there is a lot of water flowing here during part of the year?

20

A northern winter

Sigrid and her brother Leif are skiing to school in the dark! They live in a small town in the far north where the winters are very cold and dark. For part of the winter, it is dark almost all day and night. Sigrid's family and neighbors have painted their homes bright colors. This makes the village look more cheerful during the long winter months.

Sigrid's village is a long way from a city. Many of the things that people need must be brought here by boat. Sigrid's parents are expecting some supplies to arrive today. Sigrid is hoping to get a new pair of boots, and Leif needs a new jacket. Their parents have ordered some special foods to share with their friends and neighbors.

After school today, Sigrid and Leif will help their parents prepare for a neighborhood dinner. They have invited many friends to join them in a mid-winter feast. People in this community often get together for special dinners on cold winter nights.

When spring finally comes, the villagers will have a big party. There will be singing and dancing to celebrate the return of the sun.

Picture talk
Can you name the different ways the villagers travel?

Sweden's Midsummer Festival

In Sweden, after a dark, cold winter, the people like to celebrate the coming of summer. Everyone is happy that the warm weather has finally returned. This is the time of year when the days are the longest. In the northern parts of Sweden, it is light all day and night!

During the Midsummer Festival, Swedish people decorate their homes, cars, and churches with flowers and leafy branches. On the afternoon of Midsummer Eve, they gather around a pole covered with ribbons, leaves, and flowers. The decorated pole is a symbol that the growing season has begun. Winter is really over! Some people join hands and dance around the pole. Others just like to watch and clap along to the music.

Some of these people are wearing clothes that are just like ones worn long ago. *Traditional* costumes such as these remind people of their history and culture. Festivals give people a chance to carry on the customs of their ancestors.

Each year thousands of different celebrations are held all over the world. We all look forward to special occasions. When is the next festival in your community?

Picture talk

Why are flowers such an important part of this Midsummer Festival?

A Greek wedding

Stavros and Katrina got married today! Many of their friends and relatives who live in this Greek village have come to join in the celebration!

People are dancing and singing to the music of mandolins, violins, and tambourines. As the bride and groom dance, their guests come up and pin money on their clothes. Stavros and Katrina will use this money to start their new lives together.

The groom and some of the guests are wearing traditional Greek clothing. Clothes like these have been worn for hundreds of years. Nowadays they are only worn on special occasions. Some of the men are wearing baggy pants called *vraca*. The women's costumes are decorated with colorful stitching.

This wedding celebration will last for days! The guests will enjoy many delicious foods. Stavros and Katrina have made a happy beginning to their married lives.

Picture talk

Can you name at least five different ways in which flowers are used at this wedding? There are two women in the picture wearing black veils and black dresses. Why might they be dressed this way? What might the newly married couple buy with the money they are given?

Places to visit

When people visit another country, they often look forward to seeing its most famous places. Tourists like to visit the places that they have heard or read about in books. Visiting a special building or monument helps people learn about a country's history.

This is Buckingham Palace in London, England. It is the home of the Queen of England when she is in London. Every year, thousands of tourists visit Buckingham Palace. Many people like to visit this palace because it is part of England's history. The Queen's great-great grandmother, Victoria, was the first *monarch* to live in this palace.

One of the events people look forward to seeing at the palace is the changing of the guard. It takes place when the Queen is at home. As the Queen passes in her carriage, she watches the guards' routine. You can tell when the Queen is home even when she can't be seen — her special flag is flown outside!

Picture talk

There are many places around the world that attract visitors. Can you think of a special place that tourists would like to visit in your area?

Buckingham Palace is a *symbol* of England. Can you think of a symbol of another country?

27

Famous structures

Many places in the world have famous structures. You may recognize some of these. Read the lettered descriptions and match them to the numbered pictures on these pages. The answers are upside down on the opposite page.

A. This structure contains a famous bell. People in the city in which it is located set their watches by the clock that chimes in it.

B. This huge statue of a woman stands on an island in a harbor. The statue was given by France as a symbol of friendship.

C. This structure is made of white marble with many beautiful stones set in it. It was built over three hundred years ago as a tomb for an emperor's wife. It took over twenty years to build.

2. **The C.N. Tower, Toronto, Canada**

3. **The Statue of Liberty, New York, United States**

1. **The Leaning Tower of Pisa, Italy**

D. This white structure sits on the edge of a harbor. It is used for musical performances. Its roofs look like a ship's sails.

E. These huge, ancient structures were built in the desert as burial chambers for kings.

F. This structure is the tallest free-standing structure in the world. It is an important communications tower.

G. When workers built this structure long ago, it began to sink! Many years later, other people decided to finish it. When they completed it, it leaned even more! Today, the structure is still sinking slowly into the soft ground.

5. **Opera House, Sydney, Australia**

4. **Taj Mahal, Agra, India**

6. **The Great Pyramids, Egypt**

7. **Big Ben, London, England**

ANSWERS

G — 1
F — 2
E — 6
D — 5
C — 4
B — 3
A — 7

Try this. . .

Report on a country!

Each day we hear news about different countries. Hearing about life in other places can make us very curious. Pick a country that you would like to find out more about. By listening to the radio, watching the television, or reading the newspaper, write a news story about what is happening in your chosen country. Ask your friends to report on countries of their choice. When all the stories are written, take turns being newscasters!

Do some armchair traveling!

If you could travel anywhere in the world, where would you choose to go? Sometimes, when we can't actually go to a place that we are dreaming about, it is fun to read about it instead. This is called armchair traveling. You can visit other countries without ever leaving the comfort of your chair! Your teacher or school librarian can help you find books and pictures that show places you'd like to visit.

Play the souvenir game!

Souvenirs are special things we keep to remind us of places we have visited. A souvenir can be almost anything. It can be something that was bought in a store, or something that was collected on a beach or in a forest. Ask your friends to bring in a favorite souvenir or a picture of it. Get

together and, by giving one another clues, see if you can guess where the souvenirs came from!

Hands around the world

On a piece of paper, trace the outline of your hand and then cut it out. On the paper hand print your name and the name of the country that your family or ancestors have come from. Draw an outline of a map of the world, or find a wall map. Put your map on the wall and put your paper hand beside it. Take a piece of yarn or string and tack one end of it to your paper hand. Pin the other end of the piece of string to the country from which your family or ancestors have come. Ask your friends to make their own paper hands and pin them up in the same way. If you ask enough people, you'll have hands around the world!

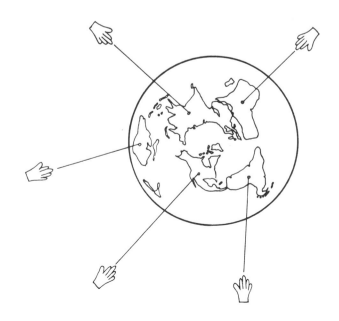

People and places dictionary

adapt   To change in order to survive new conditions or surroundings.

ancestors   The people in your family who lived long ago.

bazaar   A special sale where there are many different kinds of things to buy.

burial chamber   A special room where dead bodies are placed.

commercial   Relating to business.

community   A group of people who live in the same area and have the same government.

crew   The people who work together to sail a boat.

custom   Something that people always do. Shaking hands is a custom.

maritime   Having to do with the sea, or being near the sea.

monarch   A ruler of a country such as a king, queen, or an emperor.

moor   To tie up or anchor.

nutrients   Foods that are necessary for life and growth.

opera   A play that has most of its words sung.

oxygen   A gas that has no color and no smell, and is found in air. Plants, animals and people need oxygen to live.

poncho   A blanket with a hole in the middle. It can be worn by putting your head through the hole.

rehearsal   A practice session which is held to prepare for a performance.

resident   A person who lives in a particular place.

shear   To cut or shave off.

station   A cattle or sheep ranch.

survey   A way of gathering information that involves asking people questions.

symbol   Something that stands for, or represents, something else.

tradition   The handing down of knowledge, beliefs, and customs from one generation to the next.

tomb   A chamber in which dead bodies are placed.

tourist attraction   A place or object which interests visitors.

123456789 BP Printed in Canada 6543210987